SHOP DOGS
A photo essay of dogs that go to work.
Laurie Ross

For more information about Shop Dogs and
Laurie Ross visit: www.LaurieRossPhotography.com

10 9 8 7 6 5 4 3 2 1

Library of Congress Cataloging-in-Publication Data

ISBN: 978-0-9890031-0-0

Copyediter: Patricia Unger

 Cover and Interior Design:
Lisa Ferrante of Lisa Mia Studios
LisaMiaStudios.com

SHOP DOGS

A photo essay of dogs that go to work

LAURIE ROSS

DEDICATION

To the memory of the canine love of my life,

Abbey Girl Bonilla Ross. You taught me about love

and devotion, about being joyful "just because"

and how to laugh at myself at all times. You were

a beautiful little Vizsla and will always be in my

heart.

To all the Shop Dogs in this book and all the Shop

Dogs out there in the world. You really do make

the world a better place.

INTRODUCTION

Laurie Ross with a puppy in training at Southeastern Guide Dogs, Inc.

"Dogs make the world a better place; my goal in life is to be like my dogs and make good in the world."

One day while shopping at a granite store, I spotted Lucy, a white Great Dane lounging on a brown leather sofa. A few days later, at the gym, I met Tank, an English Bulldog puppy who was to become their "gym" dog to greet and entertain members. During my spin class, it came to me: "Shop Dogs — A Photo Essay of Dogs That Go to Work." Thus began my journey to create this book — a journey that would feed my love for dogs and encourage my passion for photographing them.

The following pages will portray many different dogs that go to work every day. They all have their own stories and have something special to say. Most are rescues and some have lived these wonderful lives since they were born. All of them have three things in common — they have a purpose and they are happy and they are completely devoted to their loved ones.

When I met Eli and Leo, I was touched by their stories. They are the Pit Bulls that work at an auto mechanic shop with their owner, Boris. Eli was rescued from a place where he was certainly on his way to a kill shelter when Boris gave him a chance. He is rewarded with Eli's complete love and devotion to Boris's entire family. Those outside Boris's family cannot go near him, as Boris describes Eli as "dangerous." Eli is at work every day (on a very thick chain) and greets customers from a distance. Leo was rescued from a backyard where he had been abandoned by his owner. Now Leo works at the shop, greets customers and allows them to pet him. Both Eli and Leo get frequent treats and Christmas presents from Boris's customers. Further reading about the joys

Remember, "There is no Psychiatrist in the world like a puppy licking your face"

- Ben Williams

and adventures of rescuing a dog can be found in the book "Buji and Me — 7 Lessons From The Dog Who Rescued Me" by Wendy Kelly.

I am also taken by the story of Brutus, a Chihuahua who works at a unique eyewear store. Brutus saved his owner's life. In her own words, Deidre writes, "I woke up one morning after a drug binge and Brutus was on top of me pawing at my face. I couldn't get sober or healthy for myself, but I couldn't say no to that little face. He loved me so much and trusted me. I couldn't let him down. Brutus totally saved my life. He had faith in me before I had faith in myself."

All of the dogs that I photographed were extraordinary, playful and inspiring. I lost track of time and place when I was with them. Although I attempted to keep the photo sessions brief, it never happened. I found myself in a joyful trance, photographing with endless enthusiasm. I know that during my short time with these pups, I was happy, at a high vibration level

and purely in a loving and peaceful place. When I felt like saying "I love you" to them, I did. No strings attached, no expectations, just pure love without condition.

There is one main theme to this adventure. In the presence of a dog, people are calmer and more social, more at ease with themselves. I'm thinking of the nursing home administrator who brings her Yorkshire Terrier, Maggie, to work with her. When I arrived for the photo session with Maggie, her owner, Migdalia, was in a staff meeting, busy planning a stressful day with staff members. Next we went to Migdalia's office, where she was on the phone comforting a concerned family member. Afterward, Migdalia sat on the floor with me while we both played with Maggie. I took photos, and Migdalia told me sweet stories and how she and the residents enjoy Maggie's company.

I'm also reminded of the little girl at the elementary school. I was photographing her teacher's dog, Homer, when she came

to me and chatted about how Homer likes her to read to him and asked if I would like to see this. Now, this was a very shy little girl who likely would not have approached me if not for Homer and their special friendship.

Barbara's dog, Lola, works in a skilled nursing facility and brings joy and love to the patients in rehabilitation. Barbara believes that "people who love animals feel emotions in an area of the brain much deeper than our everyday emotions." This observation describes the release of oxytocin, a brain chemical that produces feelings of joy and relaxation. Further reading on this concept can be found in Meg Daily Olmert's book, "Made For Each Other — The Biology of the Human-Animal Bond".

So there is no mistaking it — dogs make us better people and this is explained in the book, "Animals Make Us Human — Creating the Best Life for Animals" by Temple Grandin. When a dog is around, we're happy, feeling much less stress and are willing to engage with others due to a variety of chemical changes taking place in our blood stream. An in-depth description of this is explained in the book, "Why Zebras Don't Get Ulcers" by Robert Sapolsky. We make friends with people who have dogs, often learning the dog's name before their owner's. Dogs are true and completely devoted companions.

It has been fun for me as a photographer to see my creative vision come to life in this book. I'm truly honored to share these new friends with you. I hope you enjoy this book — the nuances, the colors, the emotions portrayed with each pup. I also hope my photographs evoke a stirring in your heart to allow your own love and creativity to shine through.

May we all shine on!!!

Laurie Ross

"He is your friend, your partner, your defender, your dog. You are his life, his leader. He will be yours, faithful and true, to the last beat of his heart. You owe it to him to be worthy of such devotion." *- Unknown*

FORWARDS

I stand in awe of Laurie Ross's amazing ability to capture the very essence of the deep bond between people and dogs. This outstandingly interesting book is packed with heart-warming essays about humans and our best friends, dogs, in a variety of intriguing work settings. The author has been honing her photographic skills for over a quarter century and this is reflected in the brilliant composition of her images, and words, in this must-have book.

Jonathan Jordan
LCSW, Animal Assisted Therapy Trainer, Business & Executive Coach

Chuck Vosburgh

Certified Professional Photographer & Educator

I first met Laurie when I was 17, where we both worked at a grocery store in St. Petersburg, Florida. I liked her dry sense of humor and even temper. When I left to start my career I never imagined we would cross paths again. Laurie is one who loves to learn and many years later she attended one of my photography classes at the Morean Arts Center in St. Petersburg. Neither of us realized we had already met, but she was one of those kind of people I immediately liked — she was soft spoken with a sharp wit. We became friends and attended many of the photography club events in the area and she attended more of my classes. Laurie's talent was very evident from the first class and it's no surprise that she has gone on to establish herself with many awards and honors and has become a well-respected photographer.

Having met her dogs, Apollo and Sophie and seeing her with them, I knew pets would play a major role in her artistic career. When Laurie told me about her idea for this book, I knew it was the perfect project for her and she was the only one who could show dogs at work in a way that goes beyond pictures and words. The photographs are beautiful and give an intimate glimpse into their daily lives. Laurie tells each dog's story which is at once unique and common to all. The reader will enjoy a real sense of the partnership between dog and human. These dogs are not only part of the family, but also an important part of the workplace. This is a book that belongs on the coffee table of every lover of dogs. The simple tones and composition combine beauty and love in a way that can be felt by anyone.

Laurie has selflessly focused on the subjects of her book, and I am pleased to be able to introduce you to her. I am honored to have been asked to write this foreword, and as I write this at my desk, my trusted dog, Lucky, is sleeping at my feet. Snoring.

This book shows something we all need in our lives, and indeed need more of. It's been a privilege working with Laurie as both friend and colleague. Who knew the girl at the grocery store would go on to create such outstanding work? I believe this will be the first of many.

Carol Zukosky

Speech Language Pathologist, Spiritual/Life Coach

The dog is the perfect mirror of devotion, play and love. Blessed by fuzzy joy and wet noses, our lives are transformed by our relationship with our canine companions. Dogs remind us no matter what, love is the only thing that matters. Laurie Ross deeply knows this heart connection as her Vizslas Sophie and Apollo know outrageous Laurie love. Through a photographic essay book of Dogs that go to work, Laurie invites us into the sweet, quirky, joy-filled world of dogs and their people. Her deep love of this animal is depicted through the language of her heart by her photographic art. We all can rest in a vision of a world where Dogs and Love are abundant and both are found at the workplace. I am delighted to invite you to enjoy the book "Shop Dogs," a creative photographic work by magnificent, loving Laurie depicting the Dogs and their people that captured her heart.

Wendy Kelly, M.Ed.

Owner & President of Pet Peeves Animal Training Inc.

I met Laurie seven years ago while working with her and her family as their animal behaviorist. It was clear to me back then, what is evident to me today. Not only is Laurie an amazing photographer, but she possesses a remarkable gift as well. Laurie does what dogs do extremely well. She has the ability to be fully present in the moment while also using her keen sense of observation to capture that moment and share with others. Laurie "shines" her light by allowing her passion for dogs to burn bright in her photographs. She mirrors that light to reflect the very best in us all as seen through the eyes of our animal companions. Shop Dogs is a heartwarming photo journal which reveals the underlying lessons that our dogs bring us throughout our workday. Our dogs remind us that the joy of doing anything in life is found in the connections we make along the way. Shop Dogs is a must read — the envy of coffee tables worldwide. So sit back, relax, and enjoy this pawsitive, photographic journey through the pages of Laurie's remarkable book.

Wendy Kelly, M.Ed. is also an Applied Animal Behaviorist Clinical Psychotherapist and Life Coach. She is the Author of "Buji and Me — 7 Lessons From The Dog Who Rescued Me", rated top 5 best reads by Modern Dog Magazine (2011 Medallion Press). She is the President and Founder of The Pawsitive Life Foundation and is an Instructor, Animal Behavior College.

Susan Wilburn

Director of Admissions & Student Services at Southeastern Guide Dogs

When invited to say something about "Shop Dogs, a Photo Essay of Dogs That Go To Work", I started to think about how essential dogs have been for humans. They have long been by our sides throughout all of recorded history and have played various roles, from hunting companions to trusted confidants and protectors.

I work with the guide dogs in training at Southeastern Guide Dogs, Inc. and get to see the impact a guide dog could have on someone's life. I never fully understood what it meant to be a team with a guide dog until my own vision loss progressed. I didn't realize my guide dog, Carson, would become an extension of me. He is part of my soul, and I his. He is so much more than a way to get around; he takes on the responsibility of my safety and allows me to be independent. Dogs are steadfast and loyal and weave themselves into our lives in ways that enrich not only our lives, but those of the people around us.

Laurie portrays this bond photographically in her book about dogs that go to work with their people. This is a beautiful photo essay of the devoted companions who are lucky to be with their people throughout the day.

MEET THE DOGS

Tank

Tank works at Spinergy Fitness with his dad, Jim Conahan, which provides cycling, boxing and personal training. Tank enjoys lifting weights, eating, sleeping and eating some more. He makes appearances throughout the day with clients and he especially likes the kids.

Breed: English Bulldog

Luke

Luke works at Suzuki Strings of St. Pete with his mom, Jennifer Diedrich. His job is to lie down, be quiet and occasionally sing along (howl) with the music. He is affectionate and energetic and is very engaging with the children in the studio. He is very good at having a calming effect on the students and is able to play the piano when prompted.

Breed: Cocker Spaniel

Vera Bradley

Vera works at Marion's, which is a ladies' clothing and gift shop owned by Marion Mitchell. Vera's job is to entertain and greet children, she "cleans" the kitchen floor and keeps the staff happy. She also knows when it's six o'clock because that's when she comes out of the office. We are never lonely here at Marion's because Vera makes every day fun.

Breed: Hungarian Vizsla

Tag

Tag works with his mom and dad, Anne and Joel Marantz at Joel Marantz Optometry. His job is to greet patients, keep opticians company and to make everyone happy. He likes to talk with the patients and this keeps everyone relaxed.

Breed: Goldendoodle
(Golden Retriever/Poodle)

Maggie Mae

Maggie works with her mom, Migdalia Santiago, at Grand Villa, an assisted living facility. She brings joy to the residents and provides a therapeutic environment for them. She mainly brings a smile to everyone's face.

Breed:

Yorkshire Terrier

Chiani & Naysa

Chiani (Italian name for The Chosen One) and Naysa (Hebrew name for Miracle of Life) work with their parents, John and Judy Grim at Haypennie Jewelers. Their job is to greet customers and to do tricks for food. They like to dance, give high fives and rollover. They get treats from the mailman and birthday cards from customers. They bring a calming effect to everyone in the store.

Breed: Half Bichon & Peekapoo

Gucci

Gucci works with her dad, Bob Barnum, at Earnest Realty, Inc. Her main job is to greet clients, supervise office employees and watch traffic. She primarily makes everyone smile!

Breed: Yorkshire Terrier

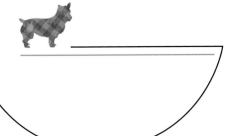

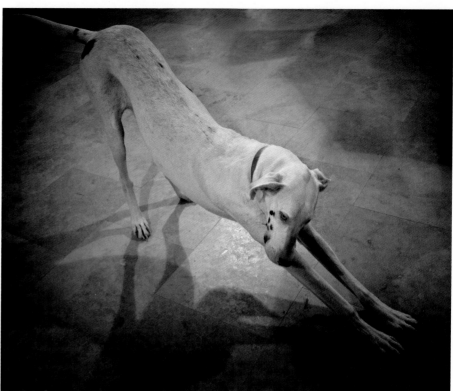

Lucy

Lucy works with her mom, Laurie Loeffler Ross, at Bayside Granite and Tiles. She is a greeter and stress reliever in the store and makes everyone smile. "She makes me feel safe, relieves my stress and it's great to have a companion with me all day!"

Breed: Great Dane

Sam "T" Kadie

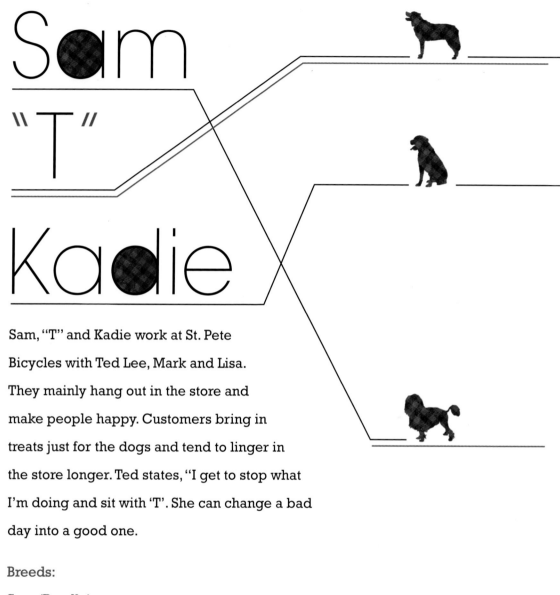

Sam, "T" and Kadie work at St. Pete Bicycles with Ted Lee, Mark and Lisa. They mainly hang out in the store and make people happy. Customers bring in treats just for the dogs and tend to linger in the store longer. Ted states, "I get to stop what I'm doing and sit with 'T'. She can change a bad day into a good one.

Breeds:

Sam (Poodle)

"T" (Akita, Shiba Inu, Terrier)

Kadie (Golden Retriever)

Willie

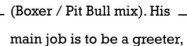

Willie works with his mom, Pamela McMasters, at Pamela M, which is a boutique for women's ready-to-wear clothing. Willie sometimes gets to work with his buddies, Sophie (Lab mix) and Lucy (Boxer / Pit Bull mix). His main job is to be a greeter, and as Pam says, "I wouldn't have it any other way."

Breed: Schnoodle (Schnauzer/Poodle)

Nick

Nick works with his mom, Diane White, at Community Support Network. He works daily to plot the overthrow of certain government officials. And when he is not bringing toys to lonely social workers, he hangs out in his bed. As Diane says, "Social work can tear your heart out. So many people need so much — having Nick at work grounds me. He helps me connect with that unconditional love one can only get from a dog. I look at him and know everything is going to be okay."

Breed: Miniature Australian Shepherd

Tank

Tank works at West Zephyrhills Elementary with his mom, Lisa Mazza. Tank is an ambassador of sorts. He greets students as they head to class in the morning. Students read to him as he approaches their desks, and everyone shares in the responsibility of having a pet in the classroom. Lisa states, "He allows me to meet so many students on campus. Tank is a conversation starter with even the shiest of students. When I walk down the hallway, everyone breaks into a smile!"

Breed: Bull Mastiff

Mini Me

Mini Me works in the counseling department at Zephyrhills Elementary School with her mom, Bridgett Crews. Students come to the office just to pet Mini Me, and soon they open up and say things like, "Did I tell you my parents are getting a divorce?" Mini Me is safe to them; they know she won't judge them. The kids can relate to her, often better than an adult. Bridgett recalls one child who wandered into her office after the death of a grandparent.

"Sometimes with Chihuahuas their eyes water up for no reason and while he was talking about his grandmother, Mini Me's eyes began to tear up." He said, "Look, Mrs. Crews, Mini Me is crying," and I asked him how he could make her feel better. He hugged her and said, "Everything is going to be all right Mini Me. Grandma is in heaven."

Breed: Chihuahua

Palin

Palin works at Zephyrhills Elementary with her mom, Linda Harris. She first greets each student as they enter the classroom every morning. As they are sitting in their seats, she goes down the line student by student and makes sure they are ready to start the day. She likes to read with them or sit on their desks while they're working. She also teaches children how to take care of a pet. Linda says that the best part of having Palin at work with her is that her presence in the classroom produces a calm atmosphere, especially if a child is having a bad day.

Breed: Poodle

Sunny

Sunny works at Zephyrhills Elementary with her mom, Kathy Kessler. She simply allows students to pet her, which helps them focus and calms them. The children also like to read to her. Kathy states, "I like to see the children relate to Sunny. She can tell when they need extra love and will go and sit beside them."

Breed: Yorkshire Terrier

Homer

Homer works at West Zephyrhills Elementary with his mom, Kathy Knox. He greets each student as they come into the classroom and is a reading buddy and a comfort giver. The best part of having Homer at work is watching the happiness and joy he shares.

Breed: Dachshund / Chihuahua

Tobias

Toby works with his dad, Mark Groutage, at Community Support Network, which is a social service provider for people in the community. He spreads the love and has a calming influence on his co-workers. His main job is to remind everyone to freely distribute treats throughout the work day.

Breed: Miniature Poodle

Emma
&
Chloe

Emma and Chloe work at Sir Speedy Printing and Marketing with their dad and mom, Jerry and Lillian Powers. Emma is a greeter, and Chloe is in charge of security. As Jerry says, "Customers and employees are nicer when the pups are around, and they have more friends than I do."

Breed: Havanese

Chad

Chad works with his dad, Jeff Schorr, at Craftsman House, which is a gallery and cafe. His two jobs at the gallery are guarding the shop and sleeping. The best part of having Chad at work is that Jeff gets to hang out all day with his best friend. A fun tidbit: Chad got his name because he was born in Florida during the 2000 presidential race (hanging chads).

Chad passed away about 6 months after these photos were taken. We find comfort in knowing he is indeed enjoying Shop Dog heaven.

Breed: Akita

Jackson Browne

Jackson works with his dad, Gregory Cahanin, at Cahanin Fire and Code, which is a fire protection engineering company. He is always ready to help at fire investigations because he makes everyone notice him. He keeps Greg company all day and they take each other on walks.

Breed: English Springer Spaniel

Jackson passed away a few months after these photos were taken. This wonderful little boy is now in Shop Dog heaven.

Guise works with his mom, Deborah Wilson, in the physical therapy department at United Therapy Group. He interacts with patients during exercise and balance activities. He plays tug to help patients

with balance and plays hide and seek with cones. The best part of having Guise at work is that he brings joy and unconditional love to a sometimes depressed and elderly population. Families of patients ask to have Guise visit their loved one daily, and patients are more likely to come to therapy knowing Guise will be there.

Breed: Labrador Retriever / Golden Retriever

Cybil & Rya

Cybil and Rya work at Hills Travel with their moms, Joan Bailey and Michelle DeVicente. Cybil is the official greeter for the travel agency. She has an instant connection to just about everyone who enters the office and presents a friendly face at Hills Travel. Rya likes to take Cybil for walks and is an overall stress reliever for everyone in the office.

Breeds:

Cybil (Chow Mix)

Rya (Mixed Breed)

Raven

Raven works at Bender's Lawn and Power Equipment with his dad and mom, Fred and Jodi Souza. Raven's main responsibility is to greet customers and to keep them entertained when the counter help is busy with other customers. "We know he's safe and comfortable when he's at work with us."

Breed: Chow / Border Collie

Baxter & Sammie

Baxter and Sammie work with their mom, Dr. GiGi, in a family practice/physician office. Dr. Gigi relates a few very touching stories about the important contributions they have made at work.

"On one occasion, a patient came to the office having a panic attack. I walked into the exam room and found her holding Baxter on his back like a baby. She told me Baxter came into the room to check on her and his presence comforted her." As she petted Baxter, her panic resolved. The patient was very thankful, convinced that Baxter was exactly what she needed.

Another patient who is deaf was having trouble coming to the office the first time to establish a new patient/doctor relationship. Baxter helped her with this visit by falling asleep in her arms while in the exam room. "She was smiling from ear to ear and was excited to tell me how Baxter helped her to feel comfortable and accepted."

As for Sammie, she's the diagnostician. A patient recently reported that Sammie entered the exam room, jumped up in her lap and stuck her nose under the patient's breast. She kept her nose there for a little while and then jumped down and left the room. "The patient never mentioned this to me, as she didn't think anything of it until two days later when she was diagnosed with a breast abscess." The patient then realized that Sammie had recognized her illness before anyone else had.

Sammie has diagnosed other patients on two different incidents as well. One time she sat at a patient's feet while looking very

worried. After the physical exam, the patient was taken to the emergency room and admitted to the hospital because she was having a heart attack. Another patient that caught Sammie's interest was unfortunately diagnosed with stage four lung cancer. "As a result, we pay very close attention to Sammie's behavior when she acts concerned or worried around patients."

Breeds:

Baxter (Bichon Mix)

Sammie (Jack Russell Mix)

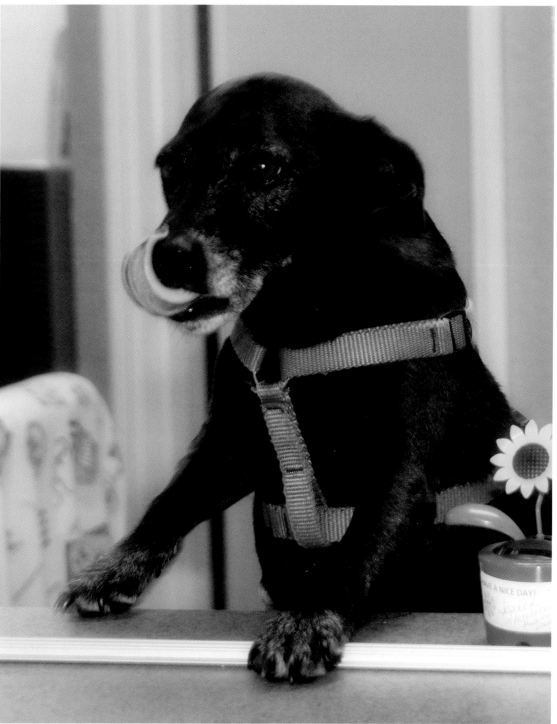

Nikki

Nikki works with her mom, Leslie Fisher, at Masthead Enterprises, a sailing store and loft. Nikki's job is to greet customers, take employees for walks, assist with lunch and supervise work in progress. "Her happy and loving spirit brings cheerfulness to the entire staff."

Breed: Belgian Sheepdog

Roscoe

Roscoe works at Shettle Family Eye Care and Eye Wear with his mom and dad, Nicole and Scott Shettle. He greets everyone and brings humor and a chuckle to all. Patients bring treats for him, but his favorite person is the UPS man. "The best part is seeing patients react to him. The children love him, and he is a good babysitter because he keeps them happy during the exams."

Breed: English Bulldog

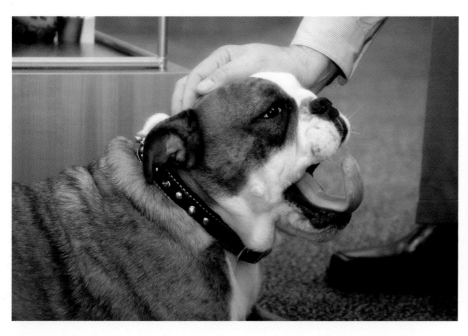

Penelope
& Lucky

Penelope and Lucky work at the dog boutique and grooming store, One Lucky Dog, with their mom, Jaime Calderbank. Their jobs are to look cute in their outfits and to sell stuff. The best part about having them at work? "I don't have to worry about them being home all alone and I get to love on them all day long."

Breeds:

Penelope (Chihuahua, Long-haired)

Lucky (Chihuahua, Short-haired)

Kacey
Lucy
Shell

Kacey, Lucy and Shell work with their dad, Michael Dunn, MD, at his physician office. They are all ice breakers for patients, they get a lot of attention and don't need to be home alone.

Breeds:

Kacey (Soft-Haired Wheaton Terrier)

Lucy (Soft-Haired Wheaton Terrier)

Shell (Chihuahua)

Fergie & Buttercup

Fergie and Buttercup work as greeters at Red Cloud Indian Arts, a retail Indian art and jewelry store, with their mom and dad, Harriet and Steve Rambeaux. Fergie has a special ability to detect Steve's mini strokes; about two hours before he has a stroke, Fergie makes a nest at Steve's side of the bed. Buttercup is a rescue from a kill shelter — one day away from her demise, she was adopted to work in the store.

Breeds:

Fergie (Airedale)

Buttercup (Wire-Haired Toy Terrier)

# Boopie

Boopie works at Goodnight Moon, a store that sells linens and children's clothes, with his mom, Jackie Powers. He is the store greeter and entertains children and bored husbands. Boopie was adopted from Florida Poodle Rescue and now works hard in the store and keeps his mom smiling.

Breed: Standard Poodle

Chloe Gucci Shylo Chanel

All four of these pups work at Positively Posh Pooch and Classy Cats Too. This is a pet boutique and grooming "spaw." Susan Nice says that Chanel and Gucci are the doggie couture models and Shylo is the guard dog and food consultant. Chloe is Dorthea Hakala's pup, and her responsibility in the shop is to play with the other dogs.

Fun boutique events that all four pups supervise include Yappy Hour (bring your pup and have a glass of wine), "Spaw" Grooming and Doggie Couture (fashion shows).

Breeds:

Chloe (Cavalier King Charles / Shih Tzu)

Gucci (Yorkshire Terrier)

Shylo (Wheaton Terrier)

Chanel (Maltese)

Eli & Leo

Eli and Leo work with their dad, Boris Intric, at Intric's Master Mechanic. Both have the job of protecting the shop and eating treats given to them by many of Boris's customers. Eli and Leo are both rescues and would simply not be alive today if it weren't for Boris. They now have fun working and are loved dearly by Boris and his family.

Breeds: Pit Bull

Dixie

Dixie works with her mom and dad, Vinita and Eric Houser, at Exotic Wood. Her three main priorities are to look pretty, greet customers and to catch up on her beauty sleep. She is well loved at home and likes being a part of all family photos. "She is an awesome dog!"

Breed: Pit Bull Mix

Pearl

Pearl works at Avrin Insurance Agency with her mom, Rebecca Avrin. She is the receptionist and greeter in the office, and Rebecca says that Pearl breaks up her day. "She gets me away from my desk to give her walks and smooches."

Breed: American Eskimo

7/Annie

Annie works in the office of psychologist Lindsay Sinclair. Annie makes everyone feel comfortable, and she especially helps kids relax when they come to the office. She dresses up for holidays, gives everyone kisses and has her own "fan club" of people who bring her treats and cards. Annie is willing to help in any way she can — she recently went with a therapist to a patient's car to help a reluctant child come in for therapy.

Breed: Cocker Spaniel

Tildie is a greeter in Mike Hopkins's dental office. She comforts patients as they come out of sedation. The entire office staff enjoys her loving spirit. "It's a joy to have her with me everyday!"

Breed: Australian Labradoodle (Labrador Retriever/Poodle)

Tildie

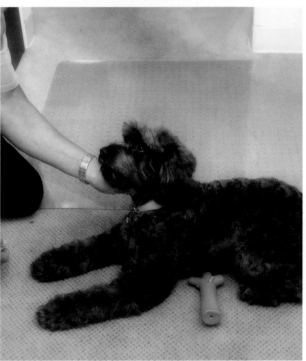

Mabel & Codie

Mabel and Codie work at Bicycle Outfitters in the retail store. Their job is to meet and greet people and to keep the children, customers and employees happy.

Breeds:

Mabel (Boxer)

Codie (Chesapeake Bay Retriever)

Buster Bojangles

Buster works with his dad, Chuck Eubanks, at Modern Optics, an eyewear and sunglass boutique. He's best at enticing people into the store and even better at accepting love from everyone. Yearly visitors from all over the U.S. and the world stop in just to say "Hi" to Buster. "His presence makes everybody happy."

Breed: French Bulldog

Max

Max works with his dad, Greg Phillips, at Gone To The Dogs, a retail and grooming store. He's best at greeting and walking around with customers. He simply makes everyone happy. "Max and I are connected when spending the day together and we get to try all the treats!"

Breed: Scottish Terrier

Scruffy

Scruffy works with his mom, Holly Kriviski, at A Point Of View, a design showroom. His job is to nip at customers who don't buy anything… Really, he is the meet-and-greet manager who licks customers when they DO spend money. "Seeing his cute, sweet face makes us all smile."

Breed: Maltese

Cooper

Cooper works with his mom and dad, Tammy and Wayne Collier, at a retail shop called Florida Jean Company. His duties include greeting the customers and entertaining the children. "He never leaves our side and won't let us leave home without him."

Breed: Yorkshire Terrier / Silky Terrier

LIVE ♥ LOVE ♥ BARK

Bandit

Bandit works at Paradise Gifts and Home Decor with her mom, Cheryl West. She meets and greets customers with her perfect manners. "Bandit is my best friend and is quite the celebrity. Customers come in asking for Bandit, but they don't know my name. They know me as Bandit's mommy and that's just fine with me!"

Breed: Doberman / Collie

Hugo & Harvey

Hugo (9 years old) and Harvey (9 months old) work with their mom, Christine, in an attorney's office. They are great stress relievers! "Hugo and Harvey keep us calm when they are mellow and make us laugh when they are playful."

Breeds: Poodle

Mango

Mango works with her mom, Caroline Saunders, at Surf Or City, a women's clothing shop. Her job in the shop is to hang back, look pretty, and share/exchange kisses. "We take dog breaks together, 10 minutes away from the floor just to snuggle."

Breed: English Mastiff

Edy

Edy works with her mom, Amy Bromley, at Being, a lifestyle store offering furniture, home accessories and gifts. She is the chief greeter and breakroom lunch companion. "I love watching Edy interact with all our customers. People are much happier with her around."

Breed: French Bulldog

MakaLe'a

MakaLe'a works with her mom, Morena Herrera, at a gift shop called Agora. The name MakaLe'a is Hawaiian for "mischievous one with twinkling eyes." She has two main jobs in the shop. First, she's the greeter, and second, she keeps husbands entertained while their wives shop. "Maka makes people relax and smile. She dresses up every day, and people are so used to seeing her this way that they will ask why she's naked when she's been out swimming or just not dressed that day."

Breed: Chinese Crested / Papillon

Jackson Manny Yoshi

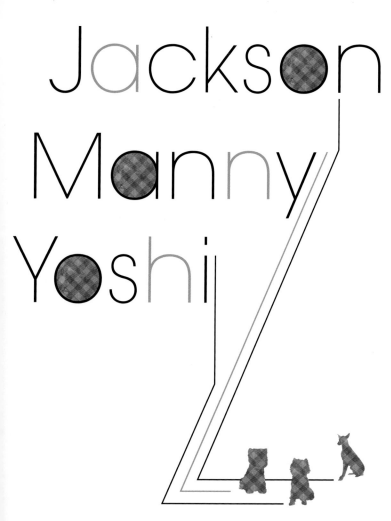

Jackson and Yoshi work with their mom, Kristen Naruns, at Northstar Realty. They both greet customers and agents, sleep, make people smile and CLOSE DEALS! Jackson is the #1 agent in the office because people come to the office just to ask if Jackson is in. "People bring them gifts, treats and toys, and they stop in just to take pictures of the boys!"

Manny works in the same office with his mom, Georgia Naruns. His first priority at work is to steal seats. Whenever anyone gets up, he jumps onto their chair. He helps to sell homes because people will stop in the office just to ask what breed of dog he is, then he talks them into buying. "Manny loves to come to work, and when the office is quiet, he just sits by me and wags his tail. In the evening when I'm working late, he will sit by the door and watch all the people walk by."

Breeds:

Jackson (Maltese / Shih Tzu)

Yoshi (Maltese / Bichon Frise)

Manny (Shiba Inu / German Shepherd)

Zorro

Zorro works with his dad, Richard Wilkes, at his legal office. His two main jobs are calming nervous visitors and doing standup comedy. "Zorro isn't home alone having a 'Ferris Bueller's Day Off' experience. Plus, he makes me laugh throughout the day."

Breed: Papillon

Sherman

Sherman works at Sweet Sage Cafe with his parents, Barbara and John Messmore. Sweet Sage is a cafe and gift shop that serves people and their dogs. Sherman's two priorities in the cafe are escorting people and their canines to their tables and making sure everyone is having a good time. He also enjoys his own dune buggy in which he and his dad ride around the beach together! "Sherman brings joy to everyone."

Some of the delights on the canine menu include French Poodle Toast, Three Dog Night (3 Beggin' Strips), These Paws Are Made For Walkin' (toast with peanut butter) and Mutt Loaf (4oz. steak ala ground). www.SweetSageCafe.com

Breed: Victorian Bulldog

118

Sir Louie Vuitton

Louie works with his mom, Vivian Spivey, at Wise Property Management. His duties include: mail delivery, paperwork courier, and checking if anyone has treats for him. "He's a great stress reliever. Everyone comes in to take a break and to give him a lot of love."

Breed: Rat Terrier

Doug

Doug is on the job at Jadus Fine Art and Portraiture with his mom, Carrie Jadus. He is a fierce guard dog, but a friendly greeter. "Doug gives me an excuse to take long walks and he is great company."

Breed: Poodle

Daisy

Daisy works with her mom, Patricia Noll, at Focus One, Inc, a mental health, drug and alcohol, and acupuncture treatment center. She has several job responsibilities, which include greeting everyone at the door. She is best at normalizing an abnormal situation for many clients, especially those who are required to attend the program by the judicial system. Daisy sits in every individual counseling session, and clients often ask to have her sit in their laps, especially when they're having a difficult time. Additionally, Daisy is involved in all group counseling sessions. Some clients want to hold Daisy prior to the group session, but they must take turns. It's normal to hear, "You held her last time" or "It's my turn to hold Daisy."

During client acupuncture treatments, Daisy lies under the treatment table. She pays special attention to every patient at the end of their treatment, as only she can do. She seems to have an inner sense for knowing what is needed. She also knows when to be quiet, automatically going from treatment room to counseling room depending upon the schedule for the day.

The best part of having Daisy with me? "We are together all day. She doesn't have to be alone. We would miss each other if we weren't working together. Plus, it's what she was born to do. She would miss the interaction with people, and those people would miss out on their interaction with her."

Breed: Maltese

Walter & Louie

Both Walter and Louie are true rags-to-riches pups. They were both rescues and now are Nuance Galleries' premier art critics. They work with their parents, Suzanne and Rob Golden, and the best part of having them in the gallery is "companionship."

Breeds:

Walter (All-American Wire Brush Scruff Hound)

Louie (Deluxe Poodle)

Maddy & Diamond

Maddy and Diamond work with their dad, William Karns, at William Karns Enterprises, a real estate developer and general contractor. Both of these boxers hang out at the office, greet clients and work as therapists at a nearby senior living facility. "We enjoy their company and companionship."

Breeds: Boxers

Riley

Riley works with her parents, Hillary and Daniel McCoy, at The Iron Pelican, an antique and home decor store. She greets customers and gives kisses when they kneel down to look at furniture. "What is better than having a beautiful Vizsla greet you? Riley is our baby and we so love bringing her to work with us, and she really enjoys it, too. She especially loves trying out the new couches!"

Breed: Hungarian Vizsla

Skippy

Skippy is the top barista at Brew D Licious where he works with his mom, Brigitte Whitaker. His main priority is to be cute all day long. "He makes everyone happy, and most people ask for Skippy before they place their coffee order."

Breed: Pomeranian Mix

Every once in a while a dog enters your life and changes everything!

Odin

Odin is top sales associate at Fig, a fine interiors / Italian linens / garden accessory retail store. He works with his mom, Marte Kehoe, greeting customers with all his cuteness. "He just gives love."

Breed: Miniature Goldendoodle
(Golden Retriever/Poodle)

Rover

Your pup will sit up pretty after his next bath. Our pet soap made with lavender, patchouli and lemongrass naturally prevents fleas and ticks... safe for humans too!

Mocha

Mocha works with her mom, Tracey DeLargy, at Milagros, a specialty soap shop. Mocha's priorities at work are sleeping / napping, looking good and guarding the shop. "Mocha is my baby and one of my best friends."

Breed: Chihuahua

Brutus

Brutus works with his mom, Deidre Wiley, at Clic, a magnetic connection eyewear store. Brutus is head of security and mostly makes everyone smile. Below, Diedre shares a very personal and inspirational story about how Brutus saved her life.

"I woke up one morning after a drug binge and Brutus was on top of me barking and pawing at my face. I was an addict and was overdosing that morning. Looking at his little face as he was trying to wake me up I decided to get sober and healthy. I couldn't say no to that little face. He loved and trusted me so much I couldn't let him down. He totally saved my life — he had faith in me before I had faith in myself."

Breed: Chihuahua

Cooper

Cooper works with his dad, Steve Busse, at Remax All Star real estate agency. His two main jobs are to be a calming influence for everyone in the office and to be the security guard. "Cooper likes being around Dad and my clients love him. He also enjoys riding in the car while I'm out showing properties."

Breed: German Shepherd

Zurco Ajax OT Vitosha

Ajax is top dog at The Dog House, LLC, which is a dog training facility. He and his mom, Carrie Silva, are a team for training many dogs from all walks of life. Ajax is particularly skilled in being a protection dog and is trained for the sport of Mondio Ring. "It's like having your best friend with you all the time."

Breed: Belgian Malinois

Katie & Reese

Katie and Reese work with their dads
at David Reynolds Jewelry and Coins.
They are best at making friends and
are great at sales. "We don't miss
them while they are at work with us
and they truly help us make friends."

Breed: Long-Haired Dachshunds

Max

Max works with his dad, Gregory Descent, at Northwest Collision Center. He is the official greeter and entertains customers by bringing his ball and stuffed puppy to show everyone. Max especially likes children and knows which delivery people bring him treats. He also knows when the mailman is due because he knows he will get a special treat from them. "It's great having Max with us at work and knowing he is never lonely is important."

Breed: Labrador Retriever, Chocolate

Peanut

Peanut works with his mom, Angela Borck, at Statement Marine, a boat manufacturer. He does his best work when begging for treats from delivery guys and when guarding the office. "Peanut is always able to be with me. I can keep an eye on him all day long."

Breed: Pomeranian

Rex works with his dad, Stefan Hoffmeister, at The Salty Dog, a do-it-yourself wash and groom shop. He is the main greeter and helps to keep the other dogs calm. "Rex is very happy to be at work with me and loves interacting with all the clients."

Breed: Standard Poodle

Rex

151

Oscar

Oscar works with his dad, Michael Bright, at Bright WoodWorks, Inc. He is a great morale booster and greets everyone with a wag of his tail. "Oscar make everyone smile."

Breed: Labradoodle (Labrador Retriever/Poodle)

George

George works with his parents at Universal Stenciling and Marking Systems, Inc. He mostly hangs out with his mom, Nancy Wright, to help her greet people and make everyone smile. George was neglected by his previous owners, so Nancy and her husband made him a part of their family. "My husband owns the company, and it can be very stressful, and it's nice to have George around because he relieves the stress. He lightens everyone's mood throughout the day."

Breed: Corgi

Lola

Lola definitely believes she is a pure breed! She goes to work daily with her mom, Barbara Lauretani, who is in charge of the therapy department at a rehab center. Lola is part of that rehab, as she serves as a much-welcomed reprieve from the challenges of the patients' injuries and illnesses. She makes them forget for just awhile that they are there for medical reasons, as her presence commands their attention and affection. She returns that love by allowing the patients to pet her, hold her and give her treats. Occasionally, she sees fit to give kisses. The facility staff is also on Lola's therapy list, as her visits with them provide a "fur fix" which allows a brief downtime from their otherwise taxing and emotionally stressful jobs.

"They say that animals are such good therapy for people for many reasons. I believe that people who love animals feel emotions in an area of the brain much deeper than our everyday emotions. In our skilled nursing facility, we may have patients who leave, then return again for various reasons. Many of them have confusion and/or dementia. They may not remember me from a previous visit nor any other staff. Sometimes they have no idea where they are. But when they see Lola, they always remember her! They may not remember her name, but they say, 'I remember that little dog.' Just that little connection can mean so much. It's guaranteed that Lola will bring a smile or a laugh to someone each and every day. I wish I could say the same for me. Lola is a special girl!"

Breed: Havanese / Shih Tzu

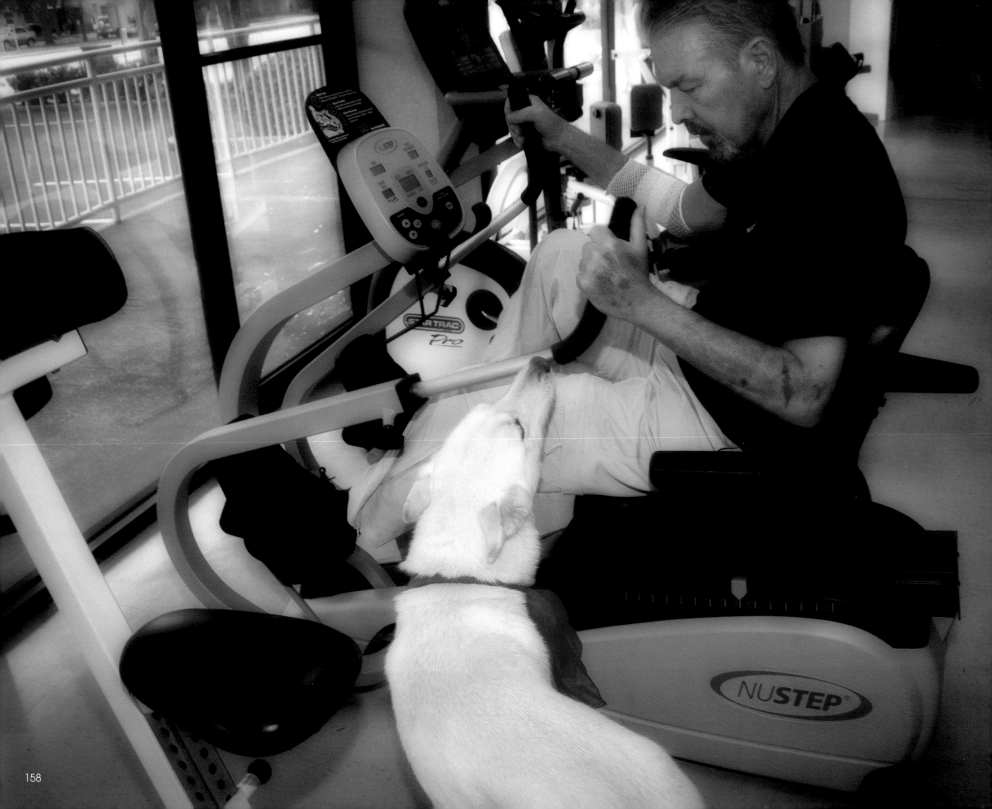

Suzie

Suzie is a recently found / rescued dog who works with her parents at Hartley Health Care. She helps her mom, Diane Hartley, give joy and comfort to all. "Suzie has a calming effect on the office and makes us all smile and laugh."

Breed: Shepherd / Husky

(One blue eye, one brown eye and six toes!)

Heinz & Bowden

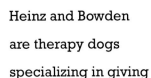

Heinz and Bowden are therapy dogs specializing in giving love and stress relief. They like to visit Stetson Law School with their mom, Diane DeDea, during the very stressful time when students are studying for the bar exam. Students are free to approach them, to love and hug them at any time. Both Heinz and Bowden like to hang out in the library to support and encourage the law students and to give sloppy good luck kisses. "They bring so much love and joy to everyone they encounter — it's so rewarding to see."

Breeds:

Heinz (Golden Retriever / Labrador Retriever)

Bowden (English Mastiff)

Brando

Brando works with his mom, Amanda Hanson, the Training Director at To The Rescue Dog Training. He helps train clients and their dogs, and he also volunteers as a therapy dog. Brando and Amanda focus their work on children and victims of domestic violence. Brando was the first therapy dog to be allowed to accompany a minor who was a victim of crime into a deposition in Florida's 6th circuit courts. He alleviates stress and provides comfort to the victims, detectives, attorneys and other witnesses. "It's wonderful being able to work with your best friend. Brando is a good ambassador for adoption and rescue (I was his 5th home by the age of 7 months) and he helps me advocate for responsible pet ownership. I also love the idea of getting your dog involved in pet volunteerism. Many causes, from beach clean ups to charity 5ks, are dog-friendly and are a great way to give back with your pet."

Breed: German Shepherd

Duncan 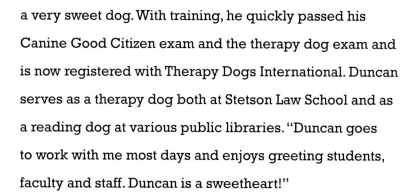 Dora James

Duncan goes to work with his dad, Pete Fitzgerald. Pete is a professor of law at Stetson Law School, where Duncan works as a therapy dog. Duncan was adopted by the Fitzgeralds in October 2009. He is a very sweet dog. With training, he quickly passed his Canine Good Citizen exam and the therapy dog exam and is now registered with Therapy Dogs International. Duncan serves as a therapy dog both at Stetson Law School and as a reading dog at various public libraries. "Duncan goes to work with me most days and enjoys greeting students, faculty and staff. Duncan is a sweetheart!"

Dora was adopted by the Fitzgeralds in November 2010 in Edinburgh, Scotland. Dora was shown in the Crufts UK dog show before being brought here to the US. "She has also passed both her canine good citizen and therapy dog exams and is a regular visitor at Stetson."

James is the most recent addition to the Fitzgerald family. He was adopted in April 2012 when he was ill and needed much medical attention. James is a great companion dog and an even better office dog. He's very popular on campus at Stetson. "Soon he will start obedience training with an eye to eventual Therapy Dog certification because he loves people of all ages. Meanwhile he is a fine traveler and a super companion!"

Breeds:

Duncan (Red Golden Retriever)

Dora (Golden Retriever, the smaller of the two blonds)

James (Golden Retriever, the larger of the two blonds)

Hans

Hans sports a tie when he comes to work with his mom, Ellen Podgor. Ellen is a professor at Stetson University College of Law. Hans is a therapy dog who comes to the library to give love and support to students who are studying for the bar exam. "Hans makes everyone smile."

Breed: Poodle

Max

Max is the greeter and fun police at Medicine River Animal Hospital. His top priority is to look cute. Max actually lives at the clinic and has the best of care and love. He was given to the clinic because he had toe cancer, and his owner, who also had cancer, could not care for him. The staff has treated Max's cancer, and he is now a happy and healthy boy. Courtney Kuntz, the main caregiver, says that Max is now cancer-free and puts a smile on everyone's face!

Max has two friends that come to work at the clinic every day. Prince is a Chinese Crested and Maya is a Chihuahua puppy.

Breed:

American Staffordshire Terrier

Tucker

Tucker works with his mom, Elizabeth Tucker, at Universal Stenciling and Marking, which is a manufacturing and assembly plant. His job is to lie around and to keep people out of Liz's workroom — unless they have her permission. "Tucker makes my workplace more stress-free and fun."

Breed: English Bulldog

Missy

Another rags to riches story... Missy sells stuff with her mom, Debbie Vandaveer, at Blue Sky Boutique. She was found in very poor condition wandering the streets, but now has a great home. Although her past is a mystery, she is well loved by Debbie and her husband, Ralph. Her job at the store is to look cute. "Who couldn't love this little fur ball?"

Breed: Shih Tzu

Dakota

Dakota works at Shapiro's Gallery with her mom, Sue Shapiro. The art gallery features contemporary craftwork, and Dakota is the door greeter. She has a happy disposition and makes people feel comfortable and relaxed. Our customers don't always remember our names, but they never forget Dakota's. The gallery sells handcrafted dog collars, as well as natural pet soaps called "shampoochie." She is a great model for the collar and has really nice, shiny fur...the pet soap is great! Bob, the UPS driver, always has cookies in his pocket for Dakota. Scott, the letter carrier is also a friend of Dakota. As soon as she hears his kickstand, she hightails it out to the gallery and eagerly awaits her treat. Shapiro's also has a loyalty program; customers are rewarded with "Dakota Dollars" that can be used towards future purchases. Dakota's face is on the "dollar"!

"Dakota is a rescue dog that found me when she was 9 months old. She's been coming to work with me for about 3 years. She's happiest when she's with me. We're both happier when we are together. The gallery is a second home for her."

Breed: Labrador Retriever

Monty works with his mom, Carol Pappas, at her medical office. He is the official office manager, greeter and the best morale booster. "We have lots of together time when he's at work with me."

Breed: Labrador Retriever

Monty

Scarlett

Ellen works with her mom, Ellen Ware, at Ware Law Group, PA. Scarlett does litigation support and is the office manager. Other job responsibilities include: taking walks, eating treats, napping, greeting clients, light chewing, researching, barking at squirrels outside the window, and napping some more. She prefers appellate work for its intellectual challenge. "Scarlett has a calming influence. She never panics in emergencies, always has something nice to say, and WORKS CHEAP!"

Breed: Cardigan Welsh Corgi

GRAND OPENING
October 1

Sarasota
Cupcake
Company

429 Corey Ave. St. Pete Beach

Sadie

Sadie is top stylist at Beach
Hair Affair, where she works
with her mom, Pat Street.
She greets customers and
performs comedy routines
for people while they wait
for services. "Sadie is fun,
and I love having her with
me all day."

Breed: Chihuahua

Sensi

Sensi works with his dad, Rasta Geary Taylor, at 1 of 1 Customs Art Gallery. He likes to greet customers and to add to the uniqueness of the store; plus, he looks good in the window. "It's amazing how much people really love Sensi. He brings happiness to people as they walk by and sometimes they come in just to love on him."

Breed: Dachshund

Blade

Blade works at Plak-It Laminating with his dad, Lonnie Shaw. He is head of security and mostly keeps busy wandering around the warehouse. He's always on high alert for customer notification. "Blade was adopted from an animal shelter and has been coming to work with me ever since."

Breed: German Shepherd

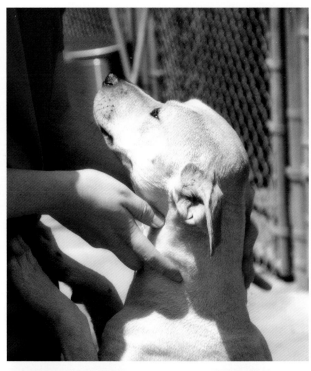

 Truly

 Nali

Savvy

Eiffel

Raven

Chrissy

All six of these dogs work with their moms at Paw In Paradise Pet Resort. Truly looks cute in the office area, Nali is the staff and client greeter, while Savvy's job is to keep everyone happy. Eiffel and Raven greet customers and hang out in day care, and Chrissy hangs out in day care and teaches social skills.

Since the taking of these photos, Chrissy has passed on. She is now in Shop Dog heaven.

Breeds:

Truly (Dachshund)

Nali (Jack Russell / Chihuahua)

Savvy (Pit Bull Mix)

Eiffel (Cane Corso)

Raven (Yorkshire Terrier Mix)

Chrissy (German Shepherd Mix)

Dakota

Dakota works with her dad, Richard Osborn, at an auto repair / muffler shop. She helps to protect the shop, and customers love hanging out with her while their car is being repaired. "Dakota is funny. She amuses the mechanics."

Breed: Puggle (Pug / Beagle)

Max & Charlie

Brothers Max and Charlie go to work with their dad, Joe Morrissey, a professor at Stetson Law School. They both make everyone relax and make students feel comfortable. They give lots of advice and remind everyone of what's important in life. "All the puppy love is the best!"

Breed: Labrador Retrievers

Sheila & Jackie "O"

Sheila and Jackie "O" are shop dogs at Owen Sweet Jewelry Design. Their job is to send out unconditional love and acceptance to all the customers who visit the gallery. They both promote a friendly environment to open communication with customers. Sheila truly enhances participation and well-being, specifically with children. Having Sheila and Jackie "O" at work helps both Owen Sweet (Sheila's dad) and Gi Gi Grimshaw (Jackie "O's" mom) to be more creative. The dogs help us put things into perspective. "To look down and see Sheila smiling at me reduces my stress level. There is no substitute for having my best friend at work with me."

Breeds:

Sheila (Toy Australian Shepherd)

Jackie "O" (Lhasa Apso / Poodle)

Athena
Stella
Holly

All three of these girls come to Stetson Law School with their mom and professor, Candace Zierdt. Their number one job is to comfort students during exam reviews. "The best part is the companionship. I don't worry about them being at home alone, and the students and I enjoy them and love their company."

Breed: Poodles

Cha Cha
Tiger
Hooch
Bruno
Spanky

Chloe
Stella
Lexi
Kodiak

All of these great dogs go to work with their moms at Joni's Pet Salon. Some are door greeters, some are ambassadors, some comfort other dogs as they come in for grooming, and others just hang out in their beds and wait to be loved and petted. "It's good for all of us to be with our dogs all day and let them play. We don't miss them when they're here with us."

There are a few cats in the salon, too. They rule the roost!

Joni's Dogs: (Top Row)

Cha Cha (Poodle)

Tiger, Hooch and Bruno (Chihuahuas)

Andrea's Dogs: (Middle Row)

Spanky (Pekingese)

Chloe (Pekingese)

Sheryl's Dogs: (Bottom Row)

Stella (Rottweiler)

Lexi (Yorkshire Terrier)

Kodiak (Affenpinscher)

Charity

Charity works with her trainer / puppy raiser, Marissa Sudweeks, at Tierra Verde Marina. Charity is a Southeastern Guide Dog (puppy) in training. The main purpose for Charity to go to work is for socialization. She also goes to restaurants, stores, schools, etc. for her to experience different sights, smells and people so she can be ready to train as a guide dog. "So many of my coworkers and customers will miss her when she's ready to go to The Southeastern Guide Dog program for further training."

Breed: Labrador Retriever

Bobby

Bobby is a hospital volunteer and therapy dog. He and his mom, Barbara Palermo, visit hospitals and give comfort to patients. He simply uses his natural talents for helping total strangers feel safe and loved with his affectionate and charming demeanor. He is also helpful and lovable to the busy hospital staff.

Barbara continues with her story:

"Bobby was a 10-month-old puppy mill dog transferred to our area by the SPCA from Montana. He was so friendly and outgoing he inspired me to get involved with rescue and volunteering. I realized after meeting many Chihuahuas that Bobby was indeed a very special dog. He is really a great ambassador for this wonderful and complex breed. The real amazing story was the transformation that started in me through Bobby. I have

suffered from major depression since I was a young child. When I was little, my true friend was the family dog. When I got Bobby, I began to walk him around the neighborhood, avoiding any and all people we would encounter. Bobby wanted to meet everyone he saw, and he taught me to be open to friends. He gives so much unconditional love and joy to all. This is why I contacted Therapy Dog International, and now he's a certified therapy dog. I tell people that he's MY therapy and this is no joke. Just before Bobby and I became volunteers in the hospital, I began falling deeper in a rut. I knew my pups were my salvation, and if I could show just how holding a furry little lover melts away pain, bitterness, sadness, and sorrow, then I could renew my soul. When Bobby gets to know you well, he smiles, stretches and "purrs" when you look in his eyes. The call from the hospital to let Bobby volunteer was a timely and special gift for me. Now we have our special "Bobby days" at the hospital, and we both feel satisfied and joyful during our visits with the patients. Thank you for letting me write about my story, Laurie. I hope you can use this in your book."

Paws Up!!!

Breed: Chihuahua

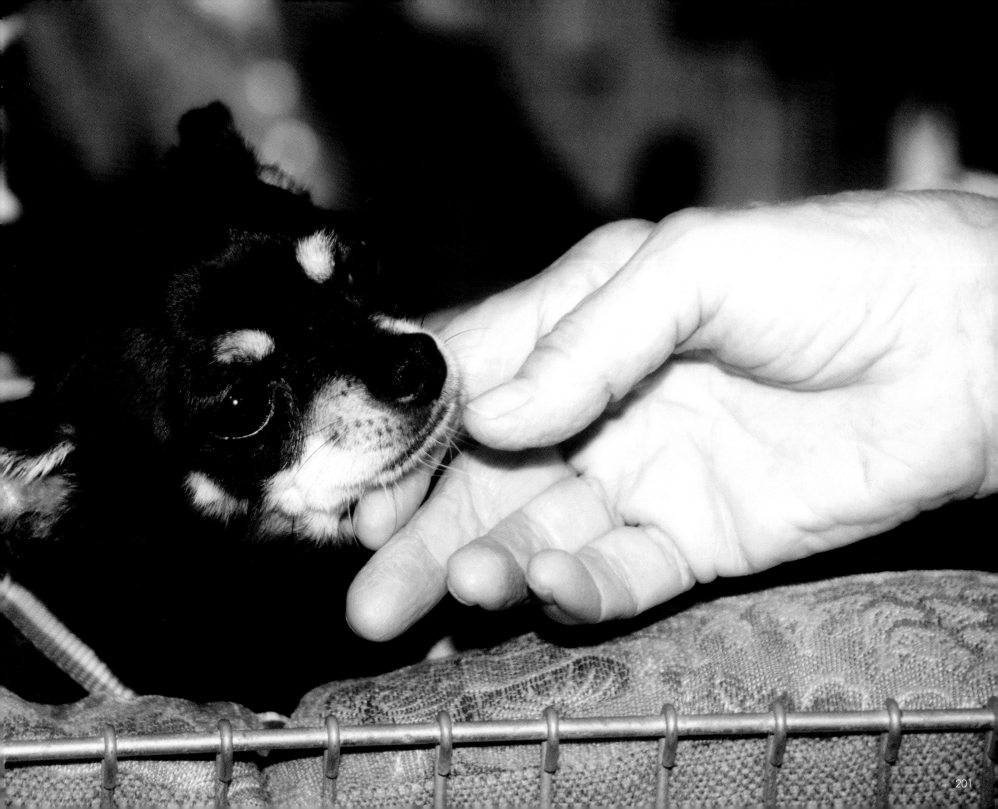

Pucci

Pucci works with her mom, Wendy Kelly, at Pet Peeves Animal Training, Inc. Wendy is an animal behaviorist working with dogs, cats, horses and birds. The best part of having Pucci at work is that she reminds everyone to connect with each other in the moment, to enjoy the journey and to be kind to all animals and their people. "Pucci teaches us to love and be loved, to belong to an energy that is greater than ourselves." Her job at the training center is to "help socialize other dogs that may have missed that opportunity and renew their trust in those silly animals called humans."

Another very important contribution Pucci brings to others is her ability to detect cancer in humans through the Paws For Life Foundation, www.Pawsitivelife.org.

Breed: Chihuahua

Sophie & Apollo

I would be remiss if I didn't include my own shop dogs in this essay!

Sophie's main job and number one priority in life is to party. She doesn't understand and will not have it if she is ignored for any length of time. She will do whatever it takes to get me to play with her or hug and kiss her throughout the day.

Apollo is a little more subdued and matter of fact. His main purpose in life is to make sure he will get his next meal in a timely manner. He will lie around and be very sweet UNTIL it gets close to when he feels he should be fed. At this point, he stands in the middle of the kitchen and barks his head off.

They are both so good to have around because they're funny and help me to remember what is important in life — partying, eating, hugging, kissing and taking long walks! I love them both with all my heart and soul!

Breed: Hungarian Vizslas

ACKNOWLEDGMENTS

Adriana Bonilla, my deepest appreciation for all your support and strength, guidance and encouragement. Thank you for your honesty, generosity and love. Your support for my creative vision is unmatched. Thank you for understanding me.

Chuck Vosburgh, I wish to express my sincere thanks to you for being there with all my questions, and for being a great teacher, mentor and, most importantly, a dear friend. I'm lucky to have you in my life and I also want you to know I am very aware of how your expertise and influence has helped me with my photography, lighting skills and editing abilities. I learned Photoshop and portrait lighting from the best, and this book would not have even begun without what I learned from you over the years.

Julia Emma Valderrama, I am extremely appreciative of your support with this endeavor and with other projects you've helped me bring to fruition. I am honored to have you in my life over the years, and I love you and your wonderful family. Thank you, Mommy!

Lisa Ferrante, thank you for designing this book. Your graphic design skills and patience with me throughout this process were very helpful. My book is beautiful because of you.

Gretchen Keehn, I'll always remember that evening at the restaurant when we chatted about what great things are happening and what can become of my book. Your vision for my project has been very clear and helpful, and I'm grateful for your organizational skills and encouragement. Thank you, my friend.

Kathy McKitchen, I'm always amazed at your patience and listening abilities. Thank you for your help with this project, for your eternal friendship and for your expertise with making me laugh; I mean really laugh!

Shannon Jones, you are a truly brilliant person. I can't thank you enough for your technical and practical advice.

To all the dogs and their people in this book who agreed to travel on this journey with me, I thank you for playing.

Carol Zukosky, Wendy Kelly, my PTA-GDO girls, Jennifer Diedrich, Jonathan Jordan, Susan Wilburn at Southeastern Guide Dogs, Laura Jaffe at Interpress Global, and the Morean Art Center have all been supportive in this endeavor.